Wakefield Press

CONFESSIONS OF AN OPERA TRAGIC

Gillian Thomas has travelled for most of her life, often alone in the early years, and frequently to Italy in pursuit of opera and a chance to speak the language.

Also a fan of Test cricket, she attends every day of every Test match at Adelaide Oval. She gets her love of sport from her father, Gordon Harris, who played 37 first class matches for South Australia between 1920 and 1931. Her love of music comes from her grandparents, who met at the Conservatorium of Music in Adelaide.

By the same author

Willingly to School

CONFESSIONS
OF AN OPERA TRAGIC

GILLIAN THOMAS

Wakefield
Press

Wakefield Press
16 Rose Street
Mile End
South Australia 5031
www.wakefieldpress.com.au

First published 2022
Reprinted 2023

Edited by Julia Beaven, Wakefield Press, and Eliza Dunn
Designed by Michael Deves, Wakefield Press
Printed in Australia by Pegasus Media & Logistics

ISBN 978 1 74305 978 4

A catalogue record for this book is available from the National Library of Australia

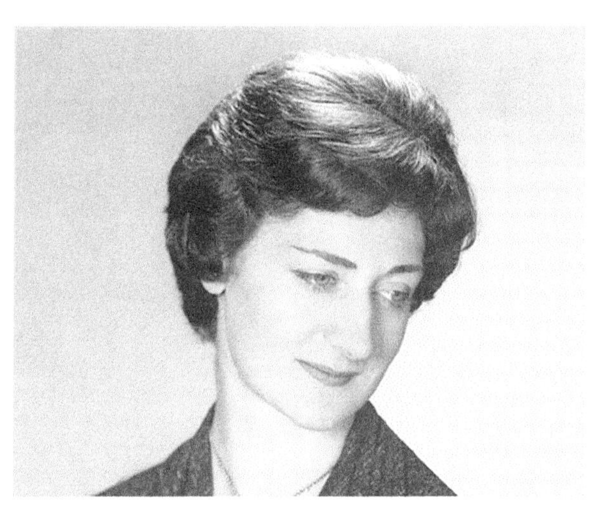

To Lauris Elms,
who swept me away

Introduction

My grandmother had been an accompanist and had met my grandfather, Wanborough Fisher, at the Elder Conservatorium of Music in Adelaide. In 1949, when I was sixteen, she gave me a ticket (E5) in the front stalls at the Theatre Royal in Rundle Street, Adelaide, for a matinee of *Tosca*.

An Italian company was touring and it was my first experience seeing an opera. My parents always listened to 5AN, the classical music station on the ABC at the time, so I probably had heard some arias on the wireless.

I was completely blown away and could not wait to see more. I begged for pocket money in advance and, with the bulk being paid by my parents, I had to sit on a ledge at the back of the gods against the back wall for ten shillings, a high price in those days as seats were usually 2/6 in the gods for operettas, etc.

The second one I saw was *Madama Butterfly*, with

Aldo Ferracuti and Mercedes Fortunata, the same soloists I'd seen in *Tosca*. In a state of near terror I found my way around to the dressing rooms to ask for autographs. I did the same thing a few nights later, after going to *Il Trovatore*. I heard the lead soprano say to a male visitor, '*Je vous remercie pour la lettre*.' As I was studying French at school I was delighted to hear and understand a sentence in the language, however short.

The next week I was there with my friend, Julienne Gunning, still on the bench leaning against the back wall. This time we were seeing *La Traviata* with Rina Mariosa, who was married to the conductor, Ermanno Wolf-Ferrari.

I do remember that after the performance the audience cheered for Rafael Lagares, who had been the tenor in *Rigoletto*, as he was about to leave next day for the Metropolitan Opera, New York. I read subsequently that he was nicknamed 'Little Caruso' because of his resemblance to Enrico.

Two years later, without being consulted, I was told by my mother that I was to have singing tuition at the Elder Conservatorium of Music as part of my education. I had no promise but my grandfather, Wanborough Fisher, had been a tenor of note in South Australia and his daughter, my aunt, Winifred Fisher, was one of the main sopranos in the ABC Wireless Chorus.

My teacher was Peter Martin and when I heard that

he and Rae Cocking were starring in Charles Gounod's *Faust* at the Hut at the Conservatorium, at Norwood Town Hall, and Port Adelaide Town Hall, I went to all three performances. I had already bought several records of the main arias, etc. so was very involved in *Faust.*

When Peter Martin moved to Queensland, I was sent to Vera Thrush at Flinders Street Baptist Church. She was invariably wearing slippers but was a very good teacher. Once I was taught by her husband, Harold Gard, when she was not well. I was terrified. He made me sing a few phrases with a match between my teeth to prove that it was possible to sing without moving one's mouth much.

He and his wife had starred in local opera performances when they were younger and she told me that he did not hold back when hurling her to the ground in *Cavalleria rusticana*. She said she was often badly bruised after a performance.

After working for three years in an insurance office to save enough money for a fare to England, I was compelled to ditch the singing lessons. I sailed to England in the *Himalaya* with a schoolfriend, Mary Auld. We were only twenty.

London, 1953

In the beginning of June, Mary and I both decided to queue in the Mall for the coronation, before looking for jobs. Arriving at 10 am the day before we must have had some stamina. We had no groundsheets, raincoats, blankets or cushions. We simply sat or lay on the hard ground. The added excitement was the announcement that Edmund Hillary had conquered Mount Everest. We did not sleep a wink and had to walk a long way to the first available women's lavatory, which was in St James's Square. I considered getting straight back in the long queue, as there would have been over seventy people in it.

In the early morning the colourful guards in their scarlet jackets lined the route, almost shoulder to shoulder. There was not much room to see between them. When it started to rain lightly, they put on their dark grey raincoats.

When the procession finally started, in very light rain, we had to remain standing and moved as far forward as possible. I remember that my feet were not still completely on the footpath and there was a mob behind always trying to get closer to the kerb. All the lovely old gold coaches were fascinating and I swear Princess Margaret met my gaze for a brief moment.

The ceremony was broadcast in its entirety so we could join in hymns and hear clearly every word spoken. At the end we dispersed with thousands of others heading for Buckingham Palace. Not having been to bed for a whole night, I recall being exhausted. It was early to bed for us when we got back to our digs.

I was woken later by a woman asking me what I was doing in her bed. Very embarrassed, I realised that when I had gone to the loo in the night I had gone into the wrong room and climbed into the wrong bed. The interesting thing was that the woman in whose bed I had been sound asleep was Joan Clements from Largs Bay, whose family ran the general store on Jetty Road and where I had often been as a small girl when staying with my grandmother in the next street.

London, 1954

I got a job at Hammer Films on Wardour Street in London. One day after work, when walking down Long Acre to buy tickets for the forthcoming *Ring Cycle*, I found myself only feet away from Joan Sutherland, in a black overcoat, heading in the same direction for a rehearsal. She was a Rhinemaiden. I paid 12/6 for a seat high in the gods, second to back row. I loved it and was thrilled to hear, for the first time, Set Svanholm as Siegfried and Margaret Harshaw as Brunnhilde. Also in the cast were Hermann Uhde, Hans Hotter and Hans Hopf. The scenery in those days was very basic, i.e. black curtain and papier-mache rock.

I frequented Sadlers Wells too. Their number one baritone was the very good-looking Dennis Dowling, a New Zealander, and their answer to Constance Shacklock was Anna Pollock. Frederick Sharp was a leading tenor and Amy Shuard the soprano. It was fabulous to go to

Covent Garden, always in the gods of course, to see James Johnson and Joan Hammond in *Aida*, and I was lucky enough to see the great Australian Sylvia Fisher in *Der Rosenkavalier* and, in other operas, Mattiwilda Dobbs and Nell Rankin.

A massive highlight was to go to Beniamino Gigli's farewell concert at the Royal Albert Hall, at which he sang twelve encores. He, the sixth son of a poor shoemaker and a teenager studying singing, would hang around kitchen doors at various hotels for possible scraps, which once contained a half-eaten scrambled egg.

I went after work to queue at the Royal Albert Hall. A girl handed in her single ticket for standing room only, which I was able to have, but then I forfeited my position in order to try to see the great man. When he came in his chauffeur-driven shiny black Daimler I had been waiting for forty minutes, but I *did* see him arrive.

There was a woman there with flowers. I heard that she always did this but he was not interested. As he pushed past the group of us we all automatically put our hands out to touch him. I then rushed up what seemed like several hundred steps to the top level.

The programme was wonderful and the three scheduled arias were from *L'Africaine*, *Carmen* and *Pagliacci*. Apart from the arranged programme, which included various Italian songs, he sang thirteen encores, of which four were arias, from *The Pearl Fishers*, *Martha*, *Aida* and *Rigoletto*.

Other encores included 'Mattinata', 'Torna Surriento', 'Mamma', 'O sole mio', and 'Ave Maria' by Bach Gounod.

The applause was indescribable. I rushed down as he was taking his last bow and found what seemed like hundreds of people waiting to see him. The woman who had the flowers tried to get into his car but two policemen hauled her out, fought with her and nearly pulled her coat off. The poor woman was screaming and almost crying.

The master then came out with a black overcoat, white scarf and homburg; he was quite red in the face after singing so much and he was coughing a bit. I clasped my hands above my head (Aussie style) to imply 'you little beauty'. He grinned and playfully shook his fist at me. The next day I sent the programme and a copy of *Music and Musicians*, which had him on the cover, to the Savoy Hotel where he was staying, and got them back, signed, by first post. I still have them.

A few weekends later, in March, June Bronhill burst on the scene at Sadler's Wells in *Die Fledermaus*. I attended with a Broken Hill boy, Gordon Foulds, who instructed me to call out 'Willyama', the Aboriginal word for Broken Hill, at the end, which I did. I'm sure she heard it amongst the tumultuous applause. That is when she took London by storm. We chatted to her afterwards, which was great fun.

After working in London for a year Mary and I set out to hitchhike a boat across the channel to Calais.

We spent one night at the Youth Hostel there and then thumbed our way to Paris in one day. We arrived so late that the hostel was full, so we had to go to a stadium on the outskirts of town where surplus hostellers were sent.

I was anxious to go to an opera and Mary did not want to go at all. So I went alone. I was feeling a little apprehensive; it was the first time that I had been on my own in a foreign country. I started with a long ride in the underground Metro, whose doors would cut you in two if you weren't quick enough.

I could be the first person ever to be eligible for the Guinness World Records for being ordered out of the Paris Opera House for wearing jeans. I had bought my ticket earlier and then had to queue for entry. A grey-haired official, who I can still see clearly in my mind, pointed with rage at my pants and screamed,

'*Pas de pantalons!*'

I could not speak French well enough to explain that I was hitchhiking and did not have a dress with me. It had been possible to wear jeans in London, as there was a separate entrance to the gods, and I often saw jeans and duffle coats. Then a man behind me in the queue came to my rescue and argued in my favour, whereupon I was allowed to proceed up the marble stairway if I did not show myself in the interval. I did, however, need to stretch my legs and did venture out of the box, which was one of those with an arch preventing you seeing more than two-thirds of the stage, unless you were sitting in the front row; in this case, I was not.

I saw three young men who I felt probably came from Adelaide, as they were wearing jackets with a band across the back at waist level as sold by a men's outfitter in Adelaide. They arranged to meet me after, to my relief, and said that they would drive me to the stadium on the outskirts of the city.

The opera was Modest Mussorgsky's *Boris Godunov*, which I had never seen before. It was an extremely hot night with no air conditioning, and I vividly remember Nicola Rossi-Lemeni taking his bow at the end, undoing his heavy fur greatcoat and gasping, '*Uffa*!'

After a refreshing *citron naturel pressé* the Adelaide boys drove me to the stadium. The walled enclosure was locked and I had not thought to advise that I would be late getting back.

There was a Norwegian boy in the same predicament and a German couple had just arrived on a motorbike. The four of us had to climb a lamppost, which was no mean feat, and then stretch over to the high wall and jump onto a nest of Dutch boy campers in small tents, who were rightfully surprised, as they had probably been asleep.

I then crept into the main building. Mary, waking, asked me if I had a nice time, to which I gasped, 'I'll tell you in the morning,' and dropped into bed, a nervous wreck.

Just over a week later we were in the Munich Youth Hostel where they would play 'Brahms' Lullaby' at 9 pm, and you were expected to go to sleep. In spite of this, some German teenagers were talking incessantly till a Melbourne girl bellowed, 'If you little bastards don't shut up I'll get the *Vater*,' which silenced them but left me trying to stifle my giggles. At 7 am we were roused by 'I love to go a-wandering' whereupon all the Germans leapt out of bed, leaving the Australians to get up later.

The main opera house in Munich was still a heap of bomb damage rubble from the war, but I found that Richard Strauss's *Die Frau ohne Schatten* was to be presented that night at the smaller Prinzregententheater with the young conductor, Rudolf Kempe. Josef Metternich was the tenor and the soprano was Marilyn Zschau.

Munich, 1954

Once again, I had not thought to tell the youth hostel that I would be going to the opera and would be late. Mary and I were therefore locked out. She had chosen to go to see the play *Dial M For Murder* and said that the only word she had understood had been 'Hallo' when someone answered the telephone.

The one place to go in the middle of the night was the railway station cafeteria, so we sat there and were joined by two GIs on leave, filling in time, as we were. We ate sausages and drank coffee for two hours until the cafeteria closed. Mary and I then walked around the streets until dawn, then waited for the youth hostel to open, so that we could get on the road again, feeling more than a little tired having not been to bed.

Vienna was our next destination, which included lunch of venison, a dish I had never eaten before in my life. Given we had been living on bread and cheese this was a nice treat. We ate at a restaurant near the autobahn and were then picked up by a bank manager.

When he said he would not be going further on the main road we were later picked up by a driver of a car registered in Paris, so we thought he was French. We rapidly discovered that we were all trying to speak school French, which was about nil. He turned out to be Frederick G. Wacker Junior, a F1 driver from Chicago who had been racing in Europe. He said that if either of us visited Chicago he would show us the photographs that had just been taken.

I sailed to Canada at the end of the year, travelling from Liverpool on the *Empress of Australia*. I worked in Toronto for a year, so I did visit Chicago one long weekend. I stayed at the YWCA and visited Frederick G. Wacker Junior in a very tall building where he had a white grand piano. He took me to lunch at the Pump Room, a very classy restaurant where I felt rather nervous, every 's' on the menu was an 'f' and the waiters were dressed from another century. Some years later I saw that Frederick was listed as one of the top ten eligible bachelors in the USA.

France, 1954

The manager was called over to meet me, as he was from Sydney, and he told me that just before I arrived the seat on which I was sitting had been occupied by one of the Gabor sisters. I don't remember if it was Zsa Zsa or Eva but I suspect the latter.

Reverting to Europe, we found the youth hostel in Vienna to be completely full and we were directed to an air-raid shelter that took surplus hostellers. We walked in, registered, and had to go along a passage and around a corner. I remember waking in the night gasping for breath and hearing Mary battling to breathe too. Of course, there were no windows, as it was all underground; the entrance was the only opening.

Mary and I had been determined to do some grape picking in France, so we headed west to a youth hostel in Saint-Aygulf. I had no watch and Mary's was broken, so as soon as the stars left the sky the first of us to wake up got up and cooked some porridge. Then, we waited on the street for a truck that would take us to Fréjus and the grape vines. At first light, we started picking.

We could not pick as fast as the tallest pickers, who were all men. We also had to wait till our lunchbreak to urinate, and go behind a tree, whereas the men simply pulled a bloomer aside when they wanted.

We experienced acute backaches but did manage to do several days of this. Everyone was entitled to a bottle of free red wine for lunch each day, but we could only manage one between us. Exhausted when we got back to the hostel, we were desperate to sleep after a light meal of spaghetti, followed by a peach each. The owner would walk around the house with a chicken under one arm and a duck under the other, which was something different. When I left the table briefly one evening the chook started on my peach, which I quickly rescued before it disappeared.

Spain, 1954

Being summer the opera houses were closed. After continuing across the south coast of France and into Spain, we saw advertising in Madrid for Donizetti's *Lucia di Lammermoor* at the Calderon Theatre. To my delight and amazement the advertised tenor was the Australian Kenneth Neate. There was one afternoon performance, so we bought tickets for that.

It was the only time that I have had uncontrollable giggles in an opera, when briefly in the blood-soaked mad scene, one of the courtiers from the chorus, with an ill-fitting orange wig, appeared to be bored stiff and gazed around waiting for his next cue while Lucia was utterly frantic. I had to stick my entire handkerchief in my mouth to stifle my hysteria.

At the conclusion, we waited at the stage door for Kenneth Neate. He was amazed to see two Aussie girls and asked us to join him for a cool drink at an outside cafe. He was in Spain to get costumes made – it was cheaper there than in other countries.

This was my last foray into opera on the trip. After Madrid, we hitched to Brittany to get to Jersey and Guernsey in the Channel Islands, and then we travelled on to England. It was not without event though, as two teenage English brothers in a small Austin picked us up and later hit, albeit not hard, a man on a bicycle who had suddenly appeared in front of us. In the 1950s there were very few cars (or bicycles) on the road.

This involved going to a courtroom in the nearest small town and waiting for a judge to come from Madrid to preside over the proceedings. I went with the older brother, aged about nineteen, as a witness, while Mary and the younger brother sat on the side of the road waiting for us to return, which we did some hours later.

I did not speak Spanish but during the court proceedings was asked what happened. I wanted to say that our car light was damaged but did not know the word for glass, so I jumped up and tapped the bare light globe hanging from the ceiling, which swung back and forth for ages.

The man claimed to have three children under five and did get a small amount of money from us, but he was not hurt at all.

When it concluded the young lawyer asked me to go out to dinner with him, an invitation I declined, of course. Even if I had been alone and free we could not have conversed at all.

When released, we headed back to the spot where Mary and the young brother had been waiting for us for hours. Then, we set off for the French border, travelling through a big town, perhaps Burgos, late at night. The people in the town were in a festive mood, with lots of people in costumes and masks milling around in the streets. It must have been Halloween.

We ended up with the car parked just off a little road in a paddock and all slept sitting up until morning.

After a few days in Jersey and Guernsey in the Channel Islands, where my father's family had come from, we arrived back in England. I left by train for Liverpool, alone, as Mary wanted a bit more time in London. I boarded the *Empress of Australia* for Canada, terminating in Montreal. Then I caught the train to Toronto the next day to start working there, for just over a year.

It was 1955. Every Saturday afternoon I listened to the broadcast from the Metropolitan Opera stage, sponsored in those days by the Texas Oil Company. It had interviews with various cast members during the intervals and an opera quiz, with commentary by Milton Cross.

Canada, 1955, and USA, 1956

In May, the Metropolitan Opera of New York paid a visit to Toronto, so at last I was able to see and hear Licia Albanese in *Madama Butterfly* and *Tosca.* I also got to see Jan Peerce, who I had idolised from my teenage years, and more recently Richard Tucker who, with Zinka Milanov and Leonard Warren, performed in *Andrea Chénier* on the same visit.

I worked in Fetterly Adjustment Service on Wellington Street in Toronto. When I told Reg Smith, a senior there, that I planned to hitch hike to New Orleans, he said, 'You could be mugged, raped or murdered.'

Nevertheless, in January 1956, I left Canada for New York, but not before I had managed to have a skiing accident at Collingwood, Ontario. The snow was starting to melt slightly and I hit, head on, the edge of a creek, which had previously been covered in snow, and I was thrown down, twisting my leg. I had to sit with my throbbing leg up in the car in which I was a passenger, all the way home. I saw a doctor the next day and was fiercely taped up and told to keep my leg up and not to get it wet.

Just days later, I was lying along the back seat of a Greyhound bus on my way to the YWCA on Lexington Avenue in New York. The bathtub there was a very ancient one on four legs. With its steep sides it was quite an exercise trying to take a bath with one leg over the side. I had to fight drowning as my head went down when my leg went up.

In those days The Metropolitan Opera was still on Broadway and I went as soon as I could to get tickets. I saw *Manon Lescaut* by Giacomo Puccini and *La forza del destino* by Giuseppe Verdi. I heard Licia Albanese in the Puccini and Zinka Milanov in the Verdi, which also had Leonard Warren and Cesare Siepi in the cast. I have since read that Forza has been notorious for being jinxed. At the Met in 1980 Leonard Warren dropped dead after singing, 'Urna fatale del mio destino,' which verges on the macabre.

I was also recently told that Siepi once asked a Scottish singer of note if he needed any help with a fencing confrontation in an opera. He thought he could handle it but in no time at all Siepi had flicked his foil out of his hand. It turned out he had represented Italy in Olympic fencing.

Leaving my case in New York I made my way to Penn Station, with only a rucksack. My first stop was at Elizabeth, New Jersey, where I sought out Nancy Jean Bowman, a girl I had met at the Paris Youth Hostel in 1954. She fed me and gave me a bed for the night, then her husband drove me early the next day to a point where I could be picked up on the Pennsylvania Turnpike. After a few minutes I got my first ride with a young man from Columbia University who had hitchhiked himself.

My next ride offered me breakfast at a restaurant. I told him I had already eaten but he insisted that I accept any free meal that was offered when hitchhiking and advised me not to hitchhike in the dark. It was the only day in my life that I have ever eaten two breakfasts and, fortified for the day ahead, I set out to the south-west into Virginia.

As the afternoon progressed, I thought it might be fun to ask at the police station in a small town if I could be locked up for vagrancy to save money on accommodation. The guy in charge was singularly disinterested in this proposition and suggested that I leave town instead, which I did.

Still in Virginia, I came to a town named Marion late in the afternoon and the staff at the police station acquiesced. Perhaps the officer thought it might teach me a lesson or relieve the boredom. They took my tiny rucksack and showed me to a cell upstairs, in which there were already two female criminals. One was chatting down a pipe to a boy below, who she later told me was convicted of murder. I was starting to feel a strong desire to get out. The lavatory had no door on it, something I had, of course, not experienced before. Until one is actually locked up one cannot imagine the feeling. Through the small window I could see that, downstairs and across the courtyard, the chief cop was going through my rucksack, looking for a gun maybe, or further identification.

On seeing this I had a great longing to scrub the adventure, so I called out for someone to come and release me. In seconds, somebody opened the heavy door and escorted me to a police car with my rucksack. I was then driven to a boarding house for the night.

Coming to the front door with a police escort, I was confronted by a large room with at least a dozen miserable and lonely looking people who could have been straight out of a Tennessee Williams play. I was taken to a spartan bedroom with army-style bed and blankets. A woman brought me a sandwich and I cried myself to sleep.

In the morning I was given a voucher to go to the Salvation Army for breakfast. I felt guilty about this and refunded the money later.

I started to hitchhike again and my driver took me into Tennessee where I was dropped on a sparsely used road before a cop in navy uniform gently ran me into a fence. He became fatherly and protective, taking me to the main road where I picked up a ride through Nashville, the state capital, and Chattanooga.

My destination that night was Tuscaloosa, Alabama, to the house of the Professor of French at the university there. I had been given his address by a friend who, several years earlier, had been a neighbour of the family in Chicago.

I arrived at his front door at 9.15 pm and I was so relieved that they took me in without a murmur, although they had no advance notice of my arrival. The professor and his wife were charming, as was the older daughter, her husband and the younger daughter, who was a schoolgirl. They gave me a meal and we talked for an hour or so. I was then given a bed and a nightgown, which was more glamorous than my pyjamas.

Tuscaloosa, and the University of Alabama, had been in the news a few weeks earlier. Autherine Lucy was the first African-American girl to attempt to go to university in Alabama. She and a friend had applied in 1952, trying to make a point and have the segregation laws changed. They had been accepted but when the university discovered they were not white they rescinded the offer. The university was legally forced to accept the girls as students in June 1955. In response, an effigy of Autherine had been burnt at the stake and a mob of more than a thousand men pelted the car in which she was driven between classes.

The next day I headed out from Tuscaloosa south-west to New Orleans, and found there was no accommodation at the YWCA. The population trebles due to the Mardi Gras, which was the reason I was there anyway, and it was hard to find a place to stay. My last driver to New Orleans did not know where the YWCA was, so I asked him to stop, having seen a teenage boy across road who I thought might know. He was black and was quite surprised that I had spoken to him.

The YWCA was inundated with women of all ages wanting accommodation. All of the women were draped on seats around the perimeter of the reception area, waiting for a bed. Luckily, several hours later, I was able to go with an older woman from Akron, Ohio, and a classy woman from Indiana who, like me, was in her twenties. She had a good sense of humour, which was handy considering we had to share the double bed. They really only wanted Catholics, so I was lucky to be there in spite of being a Protestant.

We were told there was no vacancy after that night, so I asked at a diner the next day if anyone knew of any accommodation. A man sitting on the next stool said that he would let me into his Pontiac, which was parked outside on the street. He said I could let myself in whenever I wanted and go to bed. I did exactly that and let myself out the very next morning, having slept on the back seat.

I roamed around watching parades and found that rather than the traditional Dixieland jazz, the current rhythm and blues and/or rock and roll was holding sway. On my final night I decided to 'hang out' at the bus station, prior to getting on the road to head for Florida in the morning. Having no ability to sleep sitting bolt upright in a fairly uncomfortable chair, I slept not a wink all night. During that time a guy waiting to go to Texas early in the morning was wandering around, intermittently reading comics for the entire night; then sadly, he must have fallen asleep at the last minute because he missed his bus and had another long wait.

At dawn I went out to get on the highway to Florida and promptly got a ride with two young men from Lansing, Michigan. I slept almost all day in the back seat being woken once and given a bag of chips and a bottle of Coke. We stopped the night somewhere in northern Florida in a cabin. I had a separate room, of course, but at one stage one of the boys came in with his camera to photograph me. I was fully dressed, lying on the bed reading, and told him to leave, which he promptly did. He probably wanted to record the mad Australian hitchhiker to show to his friends back in Michigan.

The next day they continued north while I stayed in Florida, hitching to Fort Lauderdale. In the one day I was picked up by a Seminole Indian and later by a gypsy, both of whom suggested that I join their camp. I declined. I ended up in West Palm Beach in a YWCA dormitory of about twenty girls. An iron was plugged into the central light fitting with an ironing board permanently ready for use beneath it. My nice driver was an insurance salesman from Union, New Jersey, who was very bored and asked me if I would like to go to the drive-in with him and see *The Man with the Golden Arm.* I had never been to a drive-in before and always enjoyed going to the pictures, so I joined him. I had not thought to tell the YWCA that I would be late. They were not impressed with me but did finally let me in.

The next day I bought a swimsuit so I could swim in the Atlantic, before setting out for Miami. I did not go to Miami Beach with all its skyscrapers and decided against attempting to get to Cuba. Being a greenhorn, and not given to buying newspapers, I had no idea that turmoil was brewing in Cuba anyway.

Heading north again, I hitched a ride with a truck driver. I had to hide in the curtained-off section behind the driver, as, near the border of South Carolina, hitchhiking is illegal. It's illegal in almost all states, although nobody seems to care much about it.

I saw a bed and breakfast sign near a small town in the late afternoon, so asked to be dropped there. Entering the sitting room, I saw an old woman in a rocking chair. She welcomed me and was all smiles until she realised that I had no car and was hitchhiking. Her expression changed immediately and she started rocking madly in her chair and asked me to leave, which I did.

Another woman, who had been in the room visiting her at the time when I arrived, followed me out of the front door and told me that her fourteen-year-old daughter lived only a few doors down the road. She was married to a seventeen-year-old boy and the woman said they would probably take me in for the night. She arranged this and I was given their double bed, sheets unchanged. I slept in my clothes.

They gave me some fried fritz for breakfast and I set off again for North Carolina. I asked my driver to set me down when I saw a bed and breakfast sign in the late afternoon. As I opened the front gate the owners of the house were walking towards me. They told me they were going to a meeting at the Baptist Church and they let me into the house, telling me to make myself at home and watch TV, as they wouldn't be back for about an hour and a half. I did not watch TV, as I had no knowledge of a TV set, so I read magazines. They returned later and were utterly charming and trusting, a far cry from the woman the night before.

A day later, I was picked up by an elderly man, with country and western music blaring. He was going fishing on the Shenandoah River and asked me if I would like to join him. Of course, I refused, but it would have been a peaceful interlude, assuming that he would not be playing cowboy songs at full volume the whole time. That ride was completely in Virginia with the Blue Ridge Mountains in sight.

In Virginia, I was picked up by white truck driver who had a black guy sitting next to him. He picked me up near the northern border, prior to entering Washington DC. He made the black bloke get out and sit on the back, dangling his legs over the edge so that I could sit at the front. This apparently alerted the police as, when we were well into Washington DC, they called us to the side of the road. I had to get out and empty my haversack on the sidewalk to be searched.

I was asked if I had a gun and I said that only a person looking for trouble would be carrying one. The cop nodded in agreement. The truck was allowed to proceed with the black guy back in front. I was left to thumb another vehicle.

I went on into Maryland and was picked up by a cop, yet again. I was taken back to the state barracks for questioning and was feeling a bit nervous at this stage. I was seated on a chair in a little room with an arc of about seven police officers staring at me. They did not believe my passport, as I had stupidly changed my signature after leaving Australia. I originally had florid loops to my name and then in England I changed to more squat letters.

When I said, 'My Gs are different,' the one in command replied, 'Your aitches are too, ma'am.' That was when they telephoned several reform institutions and found that nobody was missing. The police officer who had picked me up then returned me to the same spot and said in fatherly manner not to hitchhike in the dark. I cheekily replied, 'You have just wasted some of my daylight.'

Later, I was into New Jersey when two cops decided to interrogate me as I stood on the side of the road. They released me when I told them I was staying with friends in New Jersey then going to New York to board Cunard Line's *Queen Elizabeth.* After checking in with my friends, who were relieved to see me again, I did my laundry and had a restful day. I then took the train to New York to collect my cab to the Cunard docks. I wrongly expected tourist class to be at the back, as it had been when I sailed from Australia, but this ship, being much bigger, was able to have first and second class (the latter being eastern) while I was underneath first class. That meant, of course, that all of these cabins were below the waterline. We had a very rough patch one day where it was impossible to walk around. The wind was so strong that it blew a big wooden door off its hinges.

It was on this trip I heard that Maria Callas and Giuseppe di Stefano were just concluding a season in London – unfortunately, I would miss them by a few days. I never did see Callas, as we were never in the same place at the same time; di Stefano did, however, give a recital at the Adelaide Town Hall much later, singing gentler arias and songs.

London, 1956

Arriving in London, I went back to my digs in West Hampstead and searched for a stenography job for a couple of months before returning to Australia. A few days later I walked into the Liverpool and London Globe Insurance Company, who I had worked for in Adelaide. They said they wanted to employ me. I was almost tied to a chair and immediately asked when I could start work.

Subsequently I saw Giuseppe Verdi's *Requiem* with soloists Richard Lewis, Arda Mandikian and Scipio Colombo. I do not remember the name of the contralto, but I do recall vividly that Colombo tripped and fell flat on his face on the stage when entering, which prompted quite a lot of applause.

Tito Schipa also gave a farewell recital, which I could not miss, having been swept away after hearing *Vivere* on the radio many years before. He, at this stage, was a slightly built man, far from the larger person he had been.

Only in 2004 did I seek out his grave in a cemetery in the deep south of Italy. It was heavily wooded, with a higgledy-piggledy path, pine trees, rocks and shrubs. I could not see far from where I was and I thought I was alone until suddenly it seemed that I was about to witness a man murdering his wife. She was leaning backwards over a big boulder, and I thought he might be going to strangle her, but it turned out he had been putting in her eyedrops for her.

While I was still working in London a young Luigi Infantino was giving a concert at the Royal Festival Hall. I went to watch the tenor but was disappointed to find that it was completely sold out. As there were several of us wanting to get in, they did admit us; however, we had to sit on the stage behind him. Later in the programme he very kindly turned around and sang one of his songs to us.

At the last minute it was announced that two very important Russian visitors, Nikolai Bulganin and Nikita Kruschev, would be in London for a few days and would like to go to the Royal Ballet. It was lucky that a friend and I already had our tickets as mobs were wanting to see the Russians. The dancers were understandably trying to impress the dignitaries with their performance of *Swan Lake.* Unluckily, this may have been what caused the premier dancer to fall over at one stage.

The footpaths and roads were cordoned off by police

when we left the theatre. That was when I caught the heel of my shoe in the grating of a drain and wrestled with getting it out for what seemed like minutes, but was probably seconds – though it felt like forever with hundreds of theatregoers watching.

A short time later a season of *Tosca* was advertised to be held at the Stoll Theatre (which no longer exists). The fabulous Italian tenor Ferruccio Tagliavini would be performing. I had heard his voice on radio at home and loved it. It was the only time I have heard '*E Lucevan le stelle*' repeated after absolutely tumultuous applause. This is never supposed to happen. When waiting with a group of fans afterwards to get his autograph, he told me that I had lovely blue eyes, which had me on cloud nine all the way home.

I think it was shortly after this that Walter Midgely was brought out of retirement to do *Turandot*. This coincided with *Queen of Spades*, starring Amy Shuard, Richard Lewis, Jess Walters and Edith Coates. John Lanigan also swept me away as Pinkerton at Covent Garden. Many years later, when back in Adelaide as secretary to the State Manager of Hoyts Theatres, Alan McDowall (from Melbourne) told me that he had heard Lanigan singing in a Melbourne pub years earlier. He said he'd encouraged him to take up singing as a career, which he did with great success.

Ireland, 1956

After two months of working in Whitehall with Liverpool and London Globe Insurance, I set off to hitchhike around Ireland. It was June 1956.

With my small haversack I set out to explore the Emerald Isle. I made Stratford-upon-Avon my first stop, as Alan Badel was playing Hamlet at the theatre. I stayed at a hostel, which was almost two miles out of town, in a small neighbouring village called Ulverstone. It was very late when I got back, so I had to throw a pebble at the window upstairs to get another hosteller from the dormitory to let me in (as they close at 10 pm). I remember taking off my shoes to be quieter creeping up the stairs, but I accidentally dropped a shoe making a loud crash on the floorboards.

Although I had intended to stop at the Colwyn Bay hostel in Wales the next night it was full, so I tried two others further on, with the same result. Deciding to continue regardless, and eventually reaching Holyhead, I found there was a night ferry leaving around midnight for Dublin. This meant that I did not go to bed at all. In fact I was not even able to get a seat.

Feeling rather pale and bedraggled next morning I made my way to the youth hostel, which was in Mountjoy Square. It was still open when I arrived and I longed to go straight to bed but they were about to close for the day.

I wandered, very tired, around Dublin, bought a paperback (George Eliot's *Silas Marner*) and went to the pictures to see *Reach for the Sky*, which was so good that it commanded my complete attention and woke me up a bit.

It was June and, like most other places, the hostel was fully booked, but I was allowed to sleep on a bare mattress on the floor with four other people. My head was horribly close to a rat hole in the skirting board of the completely unfurnished and uncarpeted room. In those days, hostellers had to carry a sheet in the form of a sleeping bag, a grey blanket being available.

I discovered from an Irish friend at a Canadian Youth Hostel reunion much later that there *had*, in fact, been a rat plague in that area of Dublin in 1956, the rats coming in on Norwegian ships. She knew of this as she used to do voluntary cleaning of the hostel at the time and had lived nearby.

I hitched south to Cork next day, spent the night

there, and took a bus to Blarney Castle next morning to kiss the Blarney Stone. It was rather a hair-raising (no pun intended) experience, as I had to lie down and lean backwards over a gap high above the ground, with someone holding my knees down. I enquired as to whether the stale stains of lipstick on the stone might spread some dreadful germs and was told that the leprechauns make sure this does not happen.

I then hit the road again, heading west to the Ring of Kerry, and was fortunate to be picked up by a commercial traveller who had to make contact with various shops in the area, where he was selling bacon. He took me to a wonderful simple lunch of boiled beef and carrots at a little cafe on the way. It was almost dusk by the time I reached a hostel at Ballinskelligs Bay, where I spent the night, and I set out north next day.

Coming in to Limerick I was picked up by a teenage girl with her grandmother. The old woman asked me how I was enjoying Ireland and what I thought about the place and then handed me a rubber tube into which I had to shout at one end from the back seat to reach her barely functional ear. She still couldn't hear me so I had to raise my voice to a bellow several times. The ride was a short one within the precincts of Limerick, from where I continued north.

As I approached Killaloe, a Dr Mary Courtney of Abbey View, Killaloe, gave me a ride in a little Morris.

On arriving in the village we had to wait patiently until the drivers (one a priest) of two cars pulled together in the middle of the main road had finished their conversation. Dr Courtney took me to her home for coffee and biscuits and an interesting lesson on the history of the town, then started me on my way again.

She drove for a while on the right-hand side of the road, which alarmed me slightly, though there was scant traffic. When I asked why she was doing this she replied, 'There's a much better view of the Shannon from here.'

In 1956 there was very little traffic in Ireland. The few cars I saw were often black and usually had four or five priests inside. Other than that there were still donkey carts, which were not going very much faster than I was walking. The whitewashed walls were so pretty with purple creepers over them and it did seem a little piece of heaven.

In Galway I found everything was grinding to a halt because of the Galway race meeting. I had no experience of going to the races but decided to give it a whirl before I hunted down the hostel, which was a few miles out of the town. After a couple of hours at the races I came back to get a tram to the hostel and found that the driver and conductor had just left the tram and had also gone to the races, so I decided to walk to the hostel.

It was fully booked and, once more, I was allotted a mattress on the floor of the sitting room of the house. It was dusk at this stage and when I asked where the lavatory was I was told to go outside and through a hedge, then to my left a few yards. This was easily found but when I put my hand down to feel for a roll of toilet paper on the floor I touched a moving heap of warm feathers. It was a turkey sheltering from the wind. I leapt from the seat, dragging up my jeans and hoping not to be pecked on the bare behind.

I was lured to Connemara because I almost felt I knew the place. It was mentioned in a play called *Riders to the Sea*, which we did at my school, Girton, for the house competitions when I was fifteen. I played Bartley, the drowned son, who initially had only a few lines to say. Being a corpse is fraught with problems, however. I had to have signs of water on me so there was a bucket full of water placed in the next room near the few steps onto side stage, which was very small. I was to splash myself liberally before clambering onto a stretcher. To my horror, Pluto, the school dog, who was usually only around at lunchtimes, suddenly appeared and immediately started to lap very noisily at the water in the bucket, which caused me to have an attack of the giggles.

During rehearsals, my 'grandmother' and 'mother', keening over my body, would tickle the soles of my feet to try to destroy my equilibrium, if any, which made me determined to recite silently the Lord's Prayer in an attempt to stop myself giggling, which I did. The major difficulty was, of course, to appear to not be breathing. I did survive but was not asked to perform the following year!

Anyway, hitching in Connemara I finally found the hostel in a most beautiful position on what, to me, was almost a miniature fiord.

Before the evening meal of probably nothing much, I walked down to the landing to see the fishermen cleaning their catch. It seemed romantic at the time but next morning my boiled egg tasted horribly fishy because the chooks congregated to eat the entrails when the fish are being cleaned.

I had been too tired to go to a dance the night before in a nearby small hall but heard next morning from other hostellers that the fishermen had been dancing in Wellington boots.

On the north coast, after traversing Donegal and Londonderry, I sought out the Giant's Causeway in County Antrim. Forty thousand basalt columns rising from the sea are the result of an ancient volcanic eruption. Some of the structures tower four storeys above the water; others hardly break the surface. According to Irish myth it is part of a pathway laid to Scotland by the Irish giant, Finn McCool.

I then headed down to Newcastle and to Bloody Bridge in County Down, the latter place's colourful name being a reminder of a battle. It was a public holiday and the hostel wanted to be paid in advance but I could not get to a bank until the next day. I started to hitch back to Newcastle and thumbed a ride with a very nice woman by the name of Margie Murray, who immediately lent me one pound, which I returned to her the next day, after staying the night at Bloody Bridge youth hostel and joining the Murray family for lunch nearby at their holiday home called The Hut. Margie has since stayed with my husband and me several times, and we with her.

The final leg of my hitchhiking tour took me north to Larne to get the boat to Stranraer in Scotland.

As I left the wharf on arrival and started to walk up the road a man and his wife offered me a lift if I would help him push their car to get it started. It was the Rev. Lance Shilton from Holy Trinity in Adelaide!

My time in Ireland had been a very healthy interlude with quite a lot of walking, as most hostels seemed to be two or three miles off the main roads.

The year 2009 marked a hundred years since the start of Youth Hostels around the world, the first being in Germany.

Germany, 1956

In 1956 I hitched in Germany then flew from Hanover into Berlin, having first checked with Australia House in London if it were safe to hitchhike to Berlin through the Russian sector. I was told that it was unwise, as we had no diplomatic connections with Russia due, perhaps, to the Petrov Affair.

Berlin was on the extreme east in the communist area. This made me feel nervous on arrival at Tempelhof, as I had no knowledge of the German language, nor did I know how to get to the Youth Hostel. My kneecaps were actually shaking, something I had not experienced before, or since.

I boarded a tram and a kind woman sitting next to me told me to get off with her and not stay on the tram because the next stop was Potsdam Platz and it then went into the Russian sector. She then put me on public transport to the hostel, which was full of boys. I was the only girl.

In youth hostels one is assigned to a job of some sort and I landed one peeling potatoes in the basement with a group of teenage boy cyclists, even one from the eastern sector. We could not speak to each other of course.

The next day I was with a whole lot of schoolgirls and had to share a room with the schoolteacher in charge of them who spoke no English. She bore a remarkable likeness to a slightly terrifying one I had at school – no make up, dead straight hair, thin as a rake and sporting a full-length black leather raincoat. I respected her privacy, of course, and left the room when she was changing. Later, though, she sent me out of the room in the morning when she was discussing going to the Schiller Theatre with another teacher. I was no threat as I understood nothing and did not think it would cause a problem, even if I did know where they were going.

Being an opera tragic I sought out the Städtische Oper as the main Staatsoper was out of bounds, being in the Russian sector. This was before the wall went up. Don Pasquale was listed as being on the next afternoon so off I went. Had it been sung in Italian I would have understood some of it but it was in German and I comprehended nothing. It didn't really matter.

The next day I flew out of Tempelhof for Hamburg and eventually found my way to the Hamburg youth hostel to discover that it was completely booked out.

A French boy, about eighteen, arrived just seconds after I did and we were both instructed to go on a boat up the River Elbe to a hostel used by sailors but allowed for youth hostellers in an emergency.

The French boy, Michel, and I have exchanged Christmas cards ever since and my husband and I stayed with his family many years ago.

Coming home to Adelaide, 1956

Returning to Adelaide via the Panama Canal, I spent a lovely five weeks without having to look for a job. I was deliberately in time to go to the 1956 Olympic Games in Melbourne, where they concurrently ran a series of Mozart operas, so I went to *The Magic Flute* for the first time.

Vancouver, 1958

I returned to Adelaide to work for eighteen months, but failed to settle down. In 1958 I sailed back to Canada with the Orient Line, to Vancouver.

I worked there for a year and during that time I saw Gaetano Donizetti's *Maria Stuarda.* The opera was produced by the local company, an opera whose path I had never crossed nor did cross again. Subsequently, a Mozart opera was performed and I saw that Joan Sutherland was in it, but not in a major role. The write up praised the Canadians highly but glossed over Sutherland in a sentence or two.

Not much later she was in Italy and took La Scala by storm. She transformed into La Stupenda and had no fewer than thirty curtain calls for *Lucia di Lammermoor*. The rest, as they say, is history.

Back in Adelaide, Elizabeth Schwartzkopf gave a concert at the Adelaide Town Hall, looking and sounding absolutely wonderful. John Glennon, the reviewer from the *Sunday Mail*, was swept away by the one person being so beautiful to look at, as well as having such a beautiful voice.

In 1965, *Lucia di Lammermoor* was presented in Adelaide with Joan Sutherland. Her husband, Richard Bonynge, was the conductor. The new, young tenor singing opposite her was Luciano Pavarotti. It was a very exciting performance with such magnificent vocals, both Sutherland and Pavarotti being absolutely breathtaking.

The only clear memory I still have is of Pavarotti accidentally touching a tombstone in the graveyard. I remember it wobbling back and forth precariously.

Adelaide, 1968

Due to renovations at the Festival Theatre it was necessary for the operas to be performed at Her Majesty's on this occasion.

The leads were Marie Collier, Donald Smith and world-famous Scarpia, Tito Gobbi. Collier, always flamboyant, had reason to yank her dress from under the foot of Smith when he was on the couch having been tortured, whereupon his boot made a resounding clunk on the floor. And in the Farnese palace scene, I worried that she would be carried away putting out the candles having stabbed Scarpia. She flashed around the stage snuffing candles one-by-one, and my fear that she would accidentally put the last one out was realised. Gobbi, dead on the floor on his back, arms outstretched with a crucifix on his chest, had to die virtually in the dark.

One of the electricians from Hoyts, where I worked, was called upon to help out for the season. He told me later that Gobbi was furious. He would have performed the opera hundreds of times and I bet he didn't forget this one.

Italy, 1970

In Rome, in July, I went for the first time to the Caracalla Baths to see *Mefistofele* by Boito, whose name I had known but only as the librettist for Verdi's last two operas. I was enchanted by the music. It was a really exciting performance and I walked back to my pensione after midnight. The next night I did the same for *Aida*, which was presented with the usual array of animals on stage. The singers were not known to me at the time but it was thrilling to go to both performances under the stars on a hot summer night.

In early August a train took me to Venice where I immediately sought out the Teatro La Fenice. It was closed for the summer so I decided to go by train in the morning to Verona in case there might be an opera performed in the Arena. As luck would have it *Manon Lescaut* was to be presented that night so I immediately bought a ticket and wandered around during the day.

Luckily I had a jumper with me in spite of it being a very hot day and I used it to make sitting on a hard stone slab more comfortable.

I was amazed by the size of the orchestra pit and the stage itself. They even constructed a ship for the third act. The wonderful soprano was Magda Olivero and the tenor, whose name I did not know at the time, was a young Plácido Domingo.

Afterwards, more than ready for bed, I had instead to return to the railway station to await a train to Venice, which was not due until after 1.30 am. Luckily a farmer from Mantova sitting next to me in the waiting room offered me a strong black coffee from a flask he knew he would be needing and it 'brought me round'.

When eventually the train arrived it was completely full and I spent the entire ninety-minute trip standing in the corridor leaning on the window sill to get a breeze. I remember the man next to me saying, '*La vita è sacrificio.*'

Arriving in Venice it was necessary to find and take the ferry via the fish market, which was already open before dawn and ready for the day's sales. We called there and subsequently I left the ferry at the nearest place to Piazza San Marco, which I had to cross to get to my hotel.

I still remember the beauty of the square. It was completely empty except for one man with a straw broom sweeping the pavement underneath the arches, in each of which a round light was burning. Usually crowded with pigeons and people during the day this was a wonderful sight just before dawn.

I knocked at the hotel door, which was firmly closed, and waved my hand toward the one door key hanging on the board. The porter at first did not want to let me in. Although I had told them that I was going to the opera in Verona I don't think the information could have been passed on. Luckily he relented and I was told then that I would be able to sleep for a few hours as breakfast was served as late as 10 am.

Milan, Italy, 1972

It was Christmas Eve, 1972, late afternoon, with snow falling from the leaden sky. I had vacated my bed at 4.10 am in Adelaide, caught the first plane to Sydney, waited several hours there, then then set off via Singapore and Bangkok to Rome. On arriving I wanted to do nothing but sleep in an actual bed but I still had to transfer to the domestic terminal to fly to Milan.

Due to heavy snowfalls we had to land at yet another airport further out of Milan and take a bus to the city and then I went by taxi to my hotel.

I had booked into Marina Alla Scala, the hotel only yards from the famous opera house, and prior to creeping into bed thought that I had better drag myself to the theatre booking office to check on what was on at La Scala and when.

It was lucky that I did, as the last performance for the year was to start in three hours. I did not dare to sleep.

When going to the booking office I had noticed a big tall man in a thick overcoat wearing a wide-brimmed hat on his head at a jaunty angle, and a voluptuous woman with reddish hair, obviously singers by their deportment, walking towards the back stage door.

When I arrived in the foyer an usher dressed completely in black with knee breeches, stockings and buckles on his shoes showed me to my seat in the top balcony. I sat zombie-like under the ceiling, sucking barley sugar desperately, in near darkness. I had conflicting feelings of the awe and excitement of actually being at La Scala Milan and acute fatigue, as I swallowed yet another glucose tablet and waited for the curtains to open on *Un ballo in maschera*.

I thought the performance was wonderful, with its very bright and colourful costumes and sets, complete with elaborate chandeliers. It was a delightful way to spend Christmas Eve.

I was not familiar with any cast names other than Plácido Domingo, who was one of my favourite tenors. However, I could not be sure that the man I had seen entering at the stage door, who proved to be the tenor, was actually Domingo, as he seemed very much heavier than he had been in the only photograph I had seen of him.

Four decades later I was reading Domingo's autobiography, in which he said he was very much overweight in 1972 when singing at La Scala. So it *was* he!

On Christmas morning I had breakfast at the hotel, the only person in the dining room. I tried to coincide noisily biting into the fiendishly brittle rusks with the passing of a rattling tram where possible. I then walked through the lovely Galleria to the cathedral and sat through the sung mass twice, a special way to spend Christmas Day.

When everyone else had left I crept forward to peep at the corpse of St Carlo Borromeo, on display for Christmas in front of the altar. He lay under glass in his Cardinal's robes, his tiny hands enclosed in silk gloves. It was a slightly chilling experience to see him as he had died in 1584.

I could find no restaurant or hotel dining room open for dinner so survived on a tiny packet of cheese and biscuits I had saved from the plane. In Italy people seem to be at home with their families at Christmas, or skiing in the Alps or some such. I am sure that had I walked the mile or so to the railway station there may have been somewhere to eat but I was too tired to try.

Next day I did a tour of the city of Milan. With only two of us on the bus due to it being the day after Christmas (the other being an Indian immaculately dressed in a houndstooth overcoat and brandishing a furled umbrella) we were whizzed around the basilica of Santa Maria delle Grazie to see Leonardo da Vinci's *Last Supper*, then to Sforza Castle, the Cathedral and La Scala Theatre and Museum.

The guide, an elderly man with a very lined face and hair dyed fiercely black, said he had come from Calabria as a small boy so his father could get work. He, himself, had a good singing voice and had been a ·chorister at the cathedral and also at the Opera when children's choirs were required. He said that he was ninety and had been present at Verdi's funeral, at which Toscanini conducted the opera chorus of the Hebrew slaves from *Nabucco*, and later at Arturo Toscanini's, which I had no reason to doubt. He also used to run messages for people at La Scala as a small boy and frequently bought cigarettes for Puccini when he was there.

When I told him that I was an opera fan and Australian he took me to see a small black and white photograph of Dame Nellie Melba in the La Scala Museum. Several years later I was there again and asked if there were a photograph of Joan Sutherland, which prompted the attendant to say, 'She's not dead yet.'

After this comprehensive morning tour I finally found an automat open and ordered chicken and vegetables, but my stomach must have shrunk after eating so little since arriving and I did not want to eat much at all.

The following day on my rail pass I took the train south to Parma and checked in at the Jolly Stendhal Hotel. Once again I made my way in very cold conditions to the Opera House. I was told the theatre was completely booked out for *Un ballo in maschera* that night, this time with Jose Carreras in the lead. I was familiar with his name, as John Cargher had praised him highly as one of the up-and-coming tenors. He would perhaps have been about twenty-seven at the time.

It had been in the late 1800s that the opera fans here were so livid that a visiting tenor had to be escorted to the railway station by a horse-drawn carriage to make sure that he left town safely because he had cracked on a high note.

I begged in the booking office for them to find me a single seat somewhere. Initially they refused to do so because it was completely sold out. I said, '*Sono Australiana e sono qui specialmente di andare all'opera*,' which was true. They started mumbling between themselves and finally offered me a space on a backless bench next to a post right up under the ceiling, which I accepted with alacrity and went back to the hotel to flop on the bed for a while.

An added perk was that when having lunch in the dining room of the Jolly Stendhal Hotel I had seen the young woman who was to sing the part of Oscar in *Un ballo in maschera* sitting at the next table with her family. I had been pleasantly surprised to hear her warm up her voice only a few rooms from mine just beforehand.

It was snowing lightly when I presented myself at the Opera House that night and walked up a lot of steps to my perch. It was a great thrill to hear Jose Carreras. I walked back to my hotel after midnight in light snow and the freezing cold.

Next day I took the long trip in the train to Palermo, which involved going on the ferry across the Straits of Messina. When the ferry arrived carriages from the four railway tracks within the ferry were shunted off and those of my train shunted on. This was a fascinating experience.

I had made up my mind to go to Sicily simply because Enrico Caruso had sung at the Teatro Massimo in Palermo in the late 1800s. A rather romantic horse-drawn cab driven by a tall man with fiery red hair took me to the Grande Hotel des Palmes, where Richard Wagner had stayed when writing *Tristan and Isolde*. I was booked in looking rather strange to them in my bright blue corduroy slacks and yellow overcoat. A very superior looking employee (resembling Sir John Gielgud) who was standing near the elevator assessed me. When I said I was going to the opera, he inferred that I would have to dress up. When I appeared in my gold velvet pantsuit he nodded approval.

I walked the several blocks to the Opera House, the third largest in Europe after Paris and Moscow. It is not called Massimo for nothing.

Being early in January it was dark when I arrived and the street lights were on but as it was too early to go into the theatre I decided to walk completely around it, which was an entire block.

A tall young man in army uniform, including a greatcoat, asked if he could walk with me as he had nothing else to do. In those days there were a lot of soldiers around on national service who would be sent far from where they actually lived. He was from the north and had to serve a few months in Palermo or nearby. His English was excellent and he looked and sounded like Peter O'Toole. I remember him asking me if I had read much Kafka, to which I replied no. (I have since decided I might do so.)

Soon the doors opened and people started to arrive. I walked up the countless stairs to the entrance and was intrigued by the obligatory presence of a member of the carabinieri, in *full* regalia looking absolutely fabulous. I really felt that I was in Italy. I clambered my way up more steps to my cheaper seat in the gods for Cimerosa's *Il Matrimmonio Segreto*, which I had never seen before or since, the tenor being Luigi Alva from Argentina.

It also was my first experience hearing a claque in action for one of the female singers.

I decided to go to Trapani on the west coast the next day but did not know that only the last carriage was dropped off the train and taken by another engine due west to Trapani. The rest of us went south to Selinunte where I briefly saw an old steam engine still being used and also the visible remnants of Ancient Greece, before continuing across the bottom of Sicily and up the west coast. This took me through Mazzara and Marsala, the latter made famous by the two English brothers who started a winery there in the late 1800s. That little jaunt took all day, with a kind woman offering me an orange as she could see I had no lunch.

After two nights in Trapani, including going up to the temple on the hill on the funivia, I prepared to leave for Tunisia. I had booked a small cabin on a ship leaving very late at night. I remember that there was no drinkable water in the cabin so I swallowed an anti seasick tablet on its own. I was wearing an overcoat because it was mid winter.

I was bound for Tunis in order to visit Carthage. This was not to be. When we arrived early next morning I got down the gangplank with my case to find that I was I not allowed in the country without a visa. My travel agent at Thomas Cook had checked with Qantas who told him that I would not need one. Wrong!

I had to drag my case (before the advent of wheels) up the gangplank. The purser's office did not open so I was unable to cash a traveller's cheque.

I had no cabin and no lunch was available to me because I was not officially there. Like the Flying Dutchman I had to go where the ship was going, which was Sardinia. I stood on the deck feeling sorry for myself. Someone from the kitchen was aware of my plight and brought me a piece of octopus tentacle and a cold cooked artichoke, neither of which I had seen before in my life, but I ate them.

I had nowhere to lie down as I did not have a cabin

but the chap who had brought me the food said he had a vacant bunk in one of the cabins occupied by a woman going to Caglieri. By this time it was starting to get dark.

In the cabin was the rightful occupant, a woman who was vomiting from seasickness every few minutes. I lay facing the bulkhead to make her feel more private but the officer who had brought me there was trying to persuade her to go for a *passeggiata* with him on arrival in Caglieri. This, punctuated by throwing up, appealed to my sense of humour but I *was* sorry for her. I knew how bad it could be, having been very sick in the Great Australian Bight for several days in the *Duntroon* from Adelaide to Perth some years earlier.

Eventually we docked and I was taken off, in the dark, by someone important in the Police Department because I did not really exist. He had a very snazzy Italian car and fronted up at a hotel desk in the town only to find that the hotel was full.

We then drove a couple of miles to a resort on the coast that is usually packed to the gills in the summer but was almost empty. I was pleased to go to bed immediately but the next thing I knew I was being woken by a man coming in to the room. He was holding a bottle of beer and was very embarrassed seeing me in what he thought was his bed.

I can only think that his key probably opened the same room on the floor above. I sat up in my warm men's pyjamas and said, '*Che vuole?*' – 'What do you want?' I was eventually pleased about this as I was to sit for Matriculation Italian in a few months' time and I realised I had actually thought in Italian for the first time. The intruder apologised and disappeared.

After having some hits on a tennis court next morning with a couple of staff members I transferred to the Moderna Hotel in the city and went to a Musica Viva late afternoon 'do' there. I was amused that when the president, a woman, gave an introductory speech her voice was only near the hand-held microphone spasmodically.

Two days later I flew to Rome and became a more typical tourist.

USA, 1986

While visiting Vancouver for a reunion of Canadian youth hostellers I had known when I was working in Toronto in 1955, I also enjoyed seeing the wonderful exhibits at EXPO. I then headed south and luckily coincided with an opera season in San Francisco.

The first performance was *Il Trovatore*, where I sat near the front of the stalls at a matinee. I don't remember who the singers were. The tenor cracked on his high note which caused an elderly woman sitting behind me to yell, '*Vergogna*,' – (shame) – which I thought was very unfair. I feel only sympathy when a singer cracks on a high note.

The next night I was lucky enough to get Neil Schicoff in Don Carlos, which was simply fabulous. I had never had the opportunity to see it before and did not know that it is often sung in French, which it was on this occasion.

I continued south to stay with an English girl I had met in Palermo back in 1970. She had married an American and lived not far from Santa Barbara where I subsequently caught the train to Los Angeles.

I was talking about opera to a woman on the train and she advised me to take a cab to a hotel that catered mainly to Japanese tourists but was about four blocks from the Dorothy Chandler Pavilion where the operas were being performed – the famous auditorium where the Academy Awards were presented before moving to another theatre.

I did this and almost ran the four blocks, bought a ticket and was still panting as I got into the lift to rise to the upper circle. The opera was *Madama Butterfly* and I was not familiar with the names of the singers so don't recall them but was very glad to have been able to get in.

However, next day *Otello* by Verdi was to be presented with both Plácido Domingo and Sherrill Milnes. I could not believe my luck. When I fronted up at the booking office I found a long line of people hoping for returned tickets as the performance was completely sold out. I waited in hope for over an hour. When they reached the point of having no more tickets available I had only three people in front of me when we were told that was it. While still bemoaning my bad luck someone called out, 'Is there a single person as there is *one* seat still available?' I was very fortunate that the three people in front of me wanted to stay together.

I was thrilled to hear such famous singers and already had the record of Domingo and Milnes singing duets, including that from *Otello*. The opening scene depicting a fierce storm was stunning. I subsequently read that they had used a massive sheet of Glad Wrap, which flapped across the entire stage violently from the wings and really did look like waves.

I was happy to fly home next day to South Australia after seeing such a wonderful performance.

Italy, 1992

There were only about a dozen passengers, mopping perspiration, fanning themselves or slumped in the carriage of the cream-and-red railcar from Fidenza to Busseto in Emilia Romagna. The blinds flapped violently in the wind as we zipped along at about 70 kph in the middle of the day in the shimmering heat of the Po Valley in the first week of August.

My husband, Adrian, and I had left Geneva early that morning, changing trains at both Milano and Fidenza, and this was the last leg of our journey.

Our destination, Busseto, was the small town where Giuseppe Verdi grew up, played the organ as a boy and later lived, having been born in the nearby village of Le Roncole.

The dull yellow station building with its potted geraniums on the platform overlooked its two tracks and a dead flat view of green fields. A distant spire was just visible in the summer haze.

Within one minute of getting off the train with our two cases the other disembarking passengers had disappeared and the train had vanished in the direction of Cremona. We were alone with only the staff of three men chatting in the stationmaster's office. I had envisaged a taxi waiting but nothing was in sight anywhere and all I could hear was the dull murmur of the men in the office and the cicadas in the trees.

Il capo realised our problem and suggested that we leave our cases with him and walk up the tree-lined avenue the kilometre or so to our hotel; there was only one cab in town, he said, and it was not available for some hours.

Our hotel, I Due Foscari, was named after one of Verdi's early operas and owned by tenor Carlo Bergonzi.

Unfortunately for us he was in Siena giving a master class when we were there.

The building was utterly silent and dark with all its shutters closed against the thirty-six-degree heat. A member of the cleaning staff emerged from the gloom and gave us our key with the promise that the cab driver would be contacted and asked to collect our luggage some hours later, which did, in fact, happen. We climbed the darkened old wooden stairs, groped along the wall for the light switch and eventually found the room.

We had two days in Busseto and on the first started on foot out of the town towards Sant'Agata, about four kilometres away. The often tree-lined road wound through the flat countryside among the neatly laid-out fields of maize, most of which were higher than an elephant's eye. The only sound was the shrilling chorus of cicadas.

Passing only an occasional big house and traffic being almost nil due to it being lunch and/or siesta time, we seemed miles from anywhere until finally we saw the Sant'Agata sign to the house and the church where Verdi had worshipped.

This was the house Verdi had built for himself and Giuseppina in 1848, and to which they moved permanently two years later. It has been kept exactly as it was when Verdi lived there, and is a veritable shrine to the composer.

The high wall covered in creeper and the tall trees just inside created an air of mystery and we were about to leave in utter frustration after we found the gate tightly locked. However, two men cutting tree limbs a hundred metres away beckoned and said to ring the bell that was partly obscured and had not been noticed by us.

There was a click, the gate opened and we walked onto the gravel path leading to the house with its large terracotta pots of oleanders along the wall. A woman and her small granddaughter showed us all the ground floor rooms, some only through half-open shutters from outside, but others from the inside. We were allowed to walk into his bedroom and study. In his library we saw his opera scores, books of poetry, history and philosophy, and photographs and paintings of him, Giuseppina and their Maltese terrier Loulou. We saw the desk where he wrote, the piano he played, and finally the bed from the Milan hotel room where he died, faithfully reconstructed, together with his basin, jug and towels.

The elegant garden is very private with tall trees, ponds, statues, winding paths and occasional beds of flowers. On a little mound where Loulou was buried is the headstone. It reads: 'To the memory of one of my most faithful friends.'

The next day we visited the Villa Pallavicino in Busseto, a building from the 16th century made up of five squares, the centre being a courtyard with its crooked floor and weeds coming up between the flags, a place to catch any possible breeze. In part of this villa is the Verdi National Museum, with various relics of his life, including paintings, posters and instruments.

In the afternoon we went to the Palazzo in the Via Roma, the main street, where Verdi and Giuseppina had lived for two years prior to moving to Sant'Agata. Giuseppina in 1875 bought the building from him with a view to it being a museum to Verdi's memory, which it now is.

The guide escorting only a baritone from Birmingham with his wife and the two of us persuaded us to play the piano on which Verdi had composed *Luisa Miller* and *Stiffelio*. The temptation was too great to resist.

The Englishman, from an opera chorus, sat down and rattled off a page, sight reading from the score of *Aida*, while I managed merely an octave of the C Major scale.

Photographs and posters lined the walls including the big poster of Verdi now autographed by Ronald Pickup, who played Verdi in the television series. There was also a glass case with batons used by a number of famous conductors of his operas including, of course, Toscanini.

Next day, with train changes at Fidenza, Bologna and Firenze, we arrived at Lucca in Tuscany to pay homage to Puccini. This old walled city is bigger and more crowded with tourists than Busseto and has a museum created out of the house where Puccini lived as a boy. The museum is upstairs and houses many original Ricardi posters and photographs showing Puccini boating, riding and hunting with his publisher and editor, Giulio Ricordi.

A beautiful recording of *La Boheme* was playing as we looked at the postcards showing sequences from his operas, drawings of costume designs, his piano and a very early gramophone he had used, as well as his kitchen, dining rooms and bedroom.

From Lucca we continued on our Eurail pass to Rome for a few days then down south to Cosenza and through the Calabrian mountains on a narrow-gauge railway through countless tunnels and over bridges in very scenic countryside to Catanzaro.

We then started east to Crotone and along the sole of

the foot of Italy and gradually up the east coast, spending a night in Foggia, the birthplace of Umberto Giordano. There was a statue of him in a small park surrounded by scenes from each of his six operas, also in bronze. A slight distraction was that someone had put an empty beer can in the hand of the bronze statue.

While staying in Ancona in the Marche region north of Crotone, we went by bus one day to Beniamino Gigli's birthplace, Recanati, not far from the town of Loreto. In the municipal building in the main square is a museum of costumes he wore in the various operas in which he sang, his make-up table and photographs. His daughter was still alive at this stage and had most of his photographs. I was thrilled to have been present at his farewell concert in London. His tomb is a pyramid as his favourite opera was *Aida*. We were able to walk into it, where fresh flowers had been laid on the table.

USA, 1992

Flying to the US we checked immediately with the Met in New York and were able to get tickets for *Tales of Hoffmann* with Plácido Domingo, Carol Vaness and Samuel Ramey, conducted by James Levine. It was the opening of the season and prior to the performance a quartet from the brass section of the orchestra appeared on the balcony overlooking the Plaza and played a portion of the 'Triumphal March' from *Aida*.

There was an air of great excitement as people walked about before the main doors opened. At least eighty per cent of the men were in dinner suits or tails and there were even a couple of opera cloaks in evidence. Before the start at 7.30 everyone stood and sang the national anthem. They knew the words!

The next week we were in Chicago and able to get returned tickets on the day of the performance for Rossini's *Otello*, a beautiful production direct from

Pesaro, which we had missed by two days when we were there. Sets were very artistic and reminiscent of paintings we had seen in Urbino. It is a lovely opera, written within months of *The Barber of Seville.*

Otello was sung by Chris Merritt, dubbed 'King of the High Ds' by a New York newspaper and billed as being in the 'Eat your heart out Luciano' category. Lella Cuberli sang Desdemona and Rockwell Blake Rodrigo. In this *Otello*, Desdemona is stabbed rather than suffocated.

We were stunned by the clarity from our centrally situated box. Italian was being spoken in the box to our left and vast amounts of chocolate were being eaten in the one to the right. The opera was sung in Italian with English subtitles.

After travelling in Amtrak to St Louis we then crossed to Kansas City where we had previously arranged tickets to see *The Mikado*, performed by the Kansas City Lyric Opera. The male chorus of eight excellent singers had as much volume as you'd expect from a chorus of twenty-four.

This was perhaps the best production of *The Mikado* that we had seen. They hadn't mucked around with it. An old theatre with bare walls made for excellent acoustics, which, together with the singers' superb diction, meant not a word was missed.

Prior to the performance there was a light-hearted talk on the work in the upstairs foyer, which put people in an even more receptive frame of mind. That is now happening here.

We had booked sleepers for two nights of this trip to Los Angeles. Amtrak's Southwest Chief stops at Kansas City at 1 am and passed through the state of Kansas during the night. We had daylight in Colorado, where the buffalo still roam, and it was possible to see for some miles the wheel ruts of the old Sante Fe trail alongside the line.

We gradually gained height as we approached the Sangre de Cristo Mountains, where, though only early October, the autumn leaves had come, and sometimes gone. Our long train wound like a serpent for hours, eventually through the snow-covered Raton Pass in to New Mexico. The last of our daylight was in the station of Albuquerque, where Indians were selling their wares on the platform.

Dawn next day found us in California, where we boarded a plane and flew home via Auckland and Melbourne to Adelaide, only a few days before the season of Verdi's *Otello* at the Festival Theatre.

Wagner's Ring Cycle, Adelaide, 1998

Jeffrey Tate conducted *The Ring Cycle* performed in Adelaide in 1998. The cast included Malcolm Donnelly, Carol Yahr, David Hibbard, Edward Cook, Claire Primrose, John Keyes, John Wegner, Brian Gilbertson and Elizabeth Campbell.

Fewer than thirty-eight per cent of the audience were from South Australia, the rest being from New Zealand, Britain, Europe, South East Asia and the United States. After the performance I spoke to someone who had been sitting next to a Japanese woman in the stalls. She said that she had flown in that day and subsequently slept through the entire performance of 'Das Rheingold' and remembered nothing.

The idea to book for dinner was not a good one, though we did it for the first night. As a result of the crowd at the table for ten everyone was served only a short time before the end of the interval and, like seagulls, then rushed off to the auditorium. The second time, for 'Die Walküre' we joined a long queue at the bar for a ham roll and then had nowhere to sit to eat it. The third time I wore my red velvet pantsuit, which had big enough pockets to house a cheese sandwich on either side.

On the fourth occasion, for 'Götterdämmerung', my husband in dinner suit and I, in a long dress, walked through to North Terrace to the pie cart situated outside the Adelaide Railway Station. Two other separate blokes in dinner suits joined us as we all got stuck into pie floaters (a pie swamped in peas) standing at the counter. Rather fun.

Back in the theatre I spoke to the dinner-suited man on my right before we launched into the performance. I attempted to continue the conversation we had briefly enjoyed before going out for the dinner break but he looked a bit confused and didn't seem to know what I was talking about. It turned out that identical twins, perhaps in their late thirties, from New Zealand, were sharing the one ticket and I suddenly had a different twin next to me while the other languished out in the foyer.

Wagner's Ring Cycle No. 2, 2004

Elke Neidhardt was the producer and Asher Fisch the conductor of the 2004 performance, and Lisa Gasteen headed the stellar cast, which included Deborah Riedel, Stuart Skelton and John Wegner. A cricket bat was present on the stage sometimes to make it definitely an Australian production.

Watching 'The Ride of the Walkyries' was one of the most exciting experiences of my whole life. From the Grand Circle (alias the gods) I was agog as the bar scene was revealed glistening with silver sequins. It was incredible.

The orchestra of 120 burst upon us as one by one the Walkyries entered gleaming with silver lamé, sequined motor-bike boots and spiked hair. Three sopranos, four mezzos and a contralto, some of the best voices on the planet, belted into it and stirred us beyond description.

At the end we all, including the infirm, rose to our

feet, waved arms in the air and yelled and screamed with delight at the thrill of it all. It was bedlam. A review I read subsequently in a Melbourne paper described it as being more like a Melbourne football match crowd.

In pursuit of opera in the 200th year since the birth of Giuseppe Verdi and Richard Wagner London, 2013

Leaving Adelaide with Emirates on 15 April, I flew to London, had a couple of nights in Paddington to recover from the flight, and then took the train to Cornwall for a reunion of descendants of the forebears of my late husband. Afterward I returned to London to stay at the Strand Palace, to be near the theatres.

After the excitement of being in Westminster Abbey on Anzac Day for the memorial service, which included the Coldstream Guards (on a ticket kindly given to me by Premier Rann's chauffeur at the last minute outside the gate), I was thrilled to hear the wonderful organ. To see the Duke of Gloucester in full regalia was a nice surprise as I remembered him as a small boy in Adelaide when his father was Governor.

I went the next night to a concert of Verdi and Wagner at St Paul's Covent Garden. Allison Pearce, the singer, swept down the aisle looking very regal with a turned-up stiff gold collar on her dark grey taffeta gown, accompanied by the leading pianist from the Royal Opera House, David Syrus.

This church features in *Pigmalion* and/or *My Fair Lady* and has plaques to various famous actors and dancers on the walls, including Vivienne Leigh, Anton Dolan, Sir Robert Helpmann, Margaret Rutherford and Martita Hunt (the original Miss Haversham in the film *Great Expectations*). The last mentioned never divulged her birthdate to anyone, and the plaque has only her date of death.

A friend of mine had managed to get me a dress rehearsal ticket for *Don Carlos* to start at 11.00 on 2 May, because nothing else was available when I was in London. I was very pleased to be hearing Jonas Kaufmann in the title role.

However, my ticket was for the slips and I had not anticipated almost getting vertigo under the ceiling where I felt that I was hanging over the end of the orchestra pit, five layers up.

There are two rows in the slips. I was in the higher one, alone, with the heads of the people in front of me level with my feet. I felt exposed being the only person in the last section of five seats. There was no barrier in front of me, other than a wooden rail and a thin post to which it was attached. There were steps on one side of me, no one on the other, and I involuntarily hung on to the metal base of my seat behind the backrest. It was only possible to see the singers if they were forward on the stage.

Realising that I had the complete horrors and would have to leave, I decided to stick it out until I had heard the lovely duet between the Queen and Don Carlos. I then crept slowly and silently down the back corridor and eventually lower down in the building until I reached the foyer.

There I was placated by staff saying, 'This quite often happens,' and was told to watch a monitor in another room with a few late arrivals who were not allowed in until interval. I was then given a seat in the back of the orchestra stalls, which was wonderful. I could both see and hear. There were, however, two cameras on massive tripods in place in front of me to record the performance.

Elizabeth de Valois was sung by Anja Harteros, Princess Eboli by Béatrice Uria-Monzon and Philip II by Ferruccio Furlanetto – who had a fabulous voice and tremendous stage presence.

London, Brussels, Italy, 2013

Contenting myself with six other shows in London, I then took the Eurostar to Brussels and to the Metropole Hotel for three nights. Fresh from being a bundle of nerves in the Covent Garden slips I found myself going up to the fifth floor of this very old hotel in the last – and possibly heritage-listed – birdcage lift in Brussels, if not in Christendom. I could see through it on every side so had to close my eyes until we clanked and ground our way to a halt.

The Brussels Monnaie Theatre had ballet scheduled, so after visiting a few galleries I then continued to Milano where I did something I had never done before. I visited Casa di Riposa, Giuseppe Verdi's last resting place. On 28 February 1901, one month after the original funeral, he was moved to the completed Rest Home for Musicians. The occasion had been a state ceremony, with 200,000 people lining the black draped streets of Milan. Toscanini conducted a choir of 800 in the singing of '*Va pensiero*' from *Nabucco*.

I took a taxi there to what is now a music school and saw the tomb of Verdi and the one for his wife, in a special courtyard.

My next port of call was Busseto where Verdi had lived most of his life. He was actually born at La Roncole (from the Latin *ver roncale* – to till) just a few kilometres out of Busseto. I was able to get a bed for two nights at I Due Foscari, the little hotel where my husband and I had stayed in 1992, named after a Verdi opera first produced in 1844 and later owned by the renowned tenor Carlo Bergonzi, who died 2014.

It has only fourteen rooms and is dimly lit with all shutters on the windows tightly closed. I had to grope my way along the passage, first encountering a big cupboard, which didn't help. It had been exactly the same when my husband and I had stayed there more than twenty years earlier. They must be wanting to save on electricity bills.

I was one of only seven people there the first night and three the second, yet it was completely booked out on the third night due to there being a performance at the theatre next door. It is a quaint hotel, you feel as though you might just be on the set of *La Traviata*.

Next day I took a taxi to Roncole. When I arrived at the house where Verdi was born there was a busload of Italians from Lodi there. During the morning two further busloads, this time of Germans, arrived.

Across the road from this house is where Verdi played the organ as a boy. This village is also where Guareschi of Don Camillo fame used to live.

Steeping myself in all this, I then went to lunch in a locanda, joined by the animated crowd from the buses, who filed through the dining room where I sat. I was the only woman there and realised that I was also the sole person to have had a glass of wine, the others drinking mineral water as I think they were on a lunch break from work. Two rather sturdy fellows in white shirts and shorts and hefty boots tucked in to a large pizza each, which looked to me not much smaller than two car wheels.

I proceeded to Rome for my last three days, going straight to the Opera House to check what was on. To my delight Wagner's *Rienzi* was on that night, and almost sold out, but I was able to get a single ticket in Row D of the platea. *Rienzi* was written early in Wagner's career. I had never had the chance to see it before and doubted that I ever would again.

After a while I started to cough, unfortunately. I tried hard to stifle it but felt I should leave at the first interval. The man on my right offered me a couple of cough lozenges. It was not a cold I had but the tickle in the throat that one can get in the theatre, perhaps due to the head being tilted back a little. I asked him if there was something in the theatre that might aggravate my condition.

He said, 'Yes, it's the air conditioning.'

When I went out in the interval I discovered they had placed a large basket of cough lozenges, gratis, on the counter, so it is well known.

It was a very exciting performance and I was most impressed by the Austrian tenor, Andreas Schager, and the mezzo, the beautiful-looking Angela Denoke from Germany. The orchestra was conducted by Stefan Soltesa and there was a wonderful chorus of about seventy.

On my last night in Roma I finished with a performance of *La Traviata* by four singers and a pianist in the Sala di Congresso on Via Cavour, just seven minutes walk from my hotel.

Epilogue

I am now ninety and my love of opera is undiminished. If an upcoming Puccini – or Verdi – opera is announced, I will be there.

Wakefield Press is an independent publishing and distribution company based in Adelaide, South Australia.
We love good stories and publish beautiful books.
To see our full range of books, please visit our website at
www.wakefieldpress.com.au
where all titles are available for purchase.
To keep up with our latest releases, news and events, subscribe to our monthly newsletter.

Find us!

Facebook: www.facebook.com/wakefield.press
Twitter: www.twitter.com/wakefieldpress
Instagram: www.instagram.com/wakefieldpress